DSC SPEED READS

**PERSONAL DEVELO**

C000179130

# Time Management

## Grainne Ridge

# DIRECTORY OF SOCIAL CHANGE

Published by
Directory of Social Change
24 Stephenson Way
London NW1 2DP
Tel. 08450 77 77 07; Fax 020 7391 4804
email publications@dsc.org.uk
www.dsc.org.uk
from whom further copies and a full books catalogue are available.

Directory of Social Change is a Registered Charity no. 800517

First published 2009

ISBN 978 1 906294 22 9

British Library Cataloguing in Publication Data

A catalogue record for this book is available from the British Library

Cover and text designed by Kate Bass
Typeset by Marlinzo Services, Frome
Printed and bound by Martins of Berwick

All Directory of Social Change departments in London:
08450 77 77 07

Directory of Social Change Northern Office:
Research 0151 708 0136

# Contents

# Introduction

## Who will this book help?

Perfect time management combines complete clarity of goals, excellent personal planning skills, a positive mindset and an ability to manage external factors. This book will help anyone who is faced with a backdrop of wide-ranging choices, commitments and an ever-changing scene to manage their time effectively.

## What will it give you?

This book encourages you to look at your time management habits, both at work and at home. You will find yourself facing your long-established practices and challenging their effectiveness. While this book focuses predominantly on the work aspect, the principles and strategies apply readily to home life. Its proposed approaches draw on the wisdom of real work-life experiences and successes. They consolidate tested and accepted best practice and some forward thinking initiatives. Ultimately, this book will provide you with motivating and workable approaches to new and old challenges.

# Chapter 1

# Your time management

*This chapter provides models and techniques to help you uncover the true source of the problem.*

## Time management checklist

How do you know whether your time management is poor or not? Tick as many of these boxes that apply.

- ❏ My manager said that I needed to go on a time management course.
- ❏ I regularly miss deadlines.
- ❏ I always end up working late to finish tasks.
- ❏ I rarely complete everything on my 'to do' list.
- ❏ I lose important information.
- ❏ My friends say that I hardly ever see them.
- ❏ My children complain that I am always telling them to hurry up.
- ❏ My partner feels that I work too hard and don't spend enough time with them or the family.
- ❏ My friends always call me first.
- ❏ I find it hard to enjoy being 'in the moment'.
- ❏ I feel tired or exhausted most of the time.
- ❏ I don't find time to relax or do some exercise.
- ❏ I feel that I have no time for myself.
- ❏ There are other roles that I would like to take on but can't see where I would find the time.
- ❏ I always seem to have too much to do.
- ❏ I find it hard to decide what to tackle first.

**Top tip**

Consider the source of the problem, the impact and what will happen if you do nothing about it: simply organising tasks and commitments in the right order of priority and slavishly working through them will not necessarily deliver.

**Top tip**

Use the 'SMART' principle to help achieve your goals. This means making sure that your actions are **S**pecific, **M**easurable, **A**chievable, **R**ealistic and **T**imeframed. See page 30 for an example.

These statements are examples of symptoms which we often diagnose as poor time management. The solution is typically to prescribe a time management course where you can expect to learn how to plan, prioritise and organise your chaos.

However, look at each of the statements you've ticked and consider which categories they could fall into:

- unclear job description
- poor personal planning, prioritising and organising
- inefficient working habits
- issues with organisational structure or management
- pressure caused by others' expectations
- unrealistic expectations of yourself
- a lack of goals or standards against which to measure progress or success
- external problems impacting on your work
- liking things the way they are
- not disliking the situation enough to change it.

**Top tip**

Identify and focus on those tasks that are really important. The Pareto Principle states that roughly 80% of effects come from 20% of causes. For time management this means that 20% of your effort produces 80% of your results.

## A diagnostic tool

Here is an example: 'My manager said that I needed to go on a time management course.'

When you ask some more questions to dig deeper, you learn that your manager thinks that you need a time management course because often you cannot accommodate her late requests for information.

What is the source of the problem?

- She doesn't plan or prioritise, so action works only when it becomes urgent, even when it needs input from others; or
- I don't anticipate these requests and allow contingency time in my day in spite of my experience with her.

What is the impact of the problem?

- I feel bad about my time management skills and the perception of me which my manager holds.
- I often end up working late and feel frustrated by the lack of control that I have over the situation.
- We look like a very disorganised team.

What if I do nothing about the problem?

- Increasing frustration and dissatisfaction.
- I may even lose my job.

What are the approaches I might choose?

- I could talk to my manager about how I might be kept informed regularly of work in the pipeline which might require my input.
- I could start to build in contingency time to deal with ad hoc requests.
- I could identify the sort of information she needs and plan to have it ready whenever she asks for it.

The key to this approach is to uncover a range of options which could address the problem.

Go back to your list on page 5. Taking those statements where you put a tick in the box, use this diagnostic model to identify the key sources of your poor time management. Work through the model to identify possible approaches to address the problems. Which of these approaches would be effective and motivating?

*Diagnostic model*

| The problem: |
| The source of the problem (me/others): |
| The impact of the problem: |
| What if I do nothing? |
| Possible approaches to address it: |

**Top tip**

If someone else's disorganisation is affecting your ability to work, be assertive about it. Don't be afraid to negotiate an alternative or say 'no' to a request. If the person is resistant or won't listen, try using the 'broken record' technique. Acknowledge the comments they make, but repeat your point over and over to keep the subject on track until the person starts to hear you.

**Mike Phillips, Freelance Trainer and Consultant**

## Identifying personal development areas

**Where next?**

**www.mind tools.com**

**A website that helps you to improve your skills to further your career. Contains a useful time management section.**

It is possible to be extremely busy, to work long hours and have a wide range of time commitments outside work, yet still to feel that you are managing your time well. However, it is common to be extremely busy, work longer hours than you would like and to feel frustrated that you don't get to do the things you would like.

In both cases you're busy, but what's the real difference? In the first, you are doing what you want to do and, most importantly, have a sense of control over the time you are spending. In the second, you have lost your sense of control. You may be spending your time doing things that give no personal satisfaction.

Let's start by looking at what you are working on and how you approach it. Put a tick against each statement which is true for you (allow 10 minutes to complete).

| Area | Practice |
|---|---|
| Goals | ❏ I know what I want to achieve in the next five years.<br>❏ I know what I want to achieve in the next six months.<br>❏ I know what I want to achieve in the next week.<br>❏ I have goals in work and in other areas of my life.<br>❏ My goals are SMART, challenging and personally motivating.<br>❏ My activities today relate to my goals. |
| Know and nurture myself | ❏ I know when my energy levels are at their highest.<br>❏ I match my activities to my energy levels.<br>❏ I find time to relax and recharge my batteries.<br>❏ I find time to do some exercise.<br>❏ I find time to develop my capabilities.<br>❏ I live in the present and think about the future, rather than dwelling on what has already happened. |

| Area | Practice |
|---|---|
| Plan and prioritise | ❏  I set aside time to plan my activities weekly and daily.<br>❏  I keep a record in one place of all the tasks that I need to do.<br>❏  I estimate realistically how long each of the tasks will take.<br>❏  I allow time to get input from others where required.<br>❏  I prioritise my tasks, putting the most urgent and important at the top.<br>❏  I do tasks in order of priority, rather than those most appealing. |
| Organise myself | ❏  I can easily find information when I need it.<br>❏  When I start a task I gather all the resources I need to finish it.<br>❏  My documents are organised in a way that makes it easy for others to find information without my help.<br>❏  I always have something useful to do in unexpected spare time.<br>❏  I regularly get rid of redundant or unnecessary information, either in paper or electronic format. |
| Meetings | ❏  I involve only the relevant people in meetings (i.e. stakeholders, decision makers and contributors).<br>❏  I first set the purpose, then the agenda for each meeting.<br>❏  I share the purpose, agenda and timings with the group and gain their commitment to achieve these.<br>❏  I manage conflict and shelve irrelevant discussions.<br>❏  I ensure all actions are specific, owned and time bound.<br>❏  I only attend meetings where I can add to the discussion. |
| Decision making | ❏  I assess the need for each decision and whether I am the right person to make it.<br>❏  I distinguish between big and small decisions.<br>❏  I quickly identify and engage others who need to be involved.<br>❏  I quickly determine what information I need to make each decision and gather it.<br>❏  I set time limits on myself for making decisions.<br>❏  I use the 80:20 rule (the Pareto Principle) when making decisions. |

| Area | Practice |
|---|---|
| Media | ❏ I challenge myself to use the most effective media for each task (e.g. phone versus email, if a quick response is required).<br>❏ I cluster similar activities together (e.g. phone calls).<br>❏ I am clear about the purpose, details and next steps in my communication, whichever media I use.<br>❏ I make it clear how best to contact me and when. |
| Review | ❏ I measure what I achieve rather than how busy I am.<br>❏ I learn from experience better ways to do things.<br>❏ I review my action plan and reprioritise regularly.<br>❏ I model myself on others in my field who are excellent.<br>❏ I bin redundant activities on my 'to do' list. |
| Influence and manage others | ❏ I look for opportunities to delegate appropriately.<br>❏ I invest time in coaching the people I manage.<br>❏ I communicate well to share my expectations and to provide my team with the information they need.<br>❏ I build in time for interruptions and unexpected demands.<br>❏ I question to understand what is really needed, who is best placed to provide it and the real timescales.<br>❏ I challenge others if their requests are not reasonable and will say 'No' if required. |
| Manage crises | ❏ I quickly assess the significance of the crisis.<br>❏ I stay calm and logically determine the steps to take and by whom.<br>❏ I review each crisis and put steps in place to prevent future ones.<br>❏ I allow contingency time in my planning to deal with crises. |

**Top tip**

If you don't know how you are spending time, keep an activity log.

Highlight the individual statements with no tick.

Rank these statements in order of importance, where '1' is the activity which would improve your time management the most, '2' the next and so on. Keep this list in mind for action planning in chapter 5.

While the emphasis in this book is on work habits, many of these techniques apply in our roles outside work.

# Chapter 2

# Goal-setting for success

*This chapter looks at the power of goals in changing entrenched time management habits. It covers the benefits, assesses your roles and goals, gives some strategies for setting goals and explores your personal motivation to achieve them.*

How many New Year's resolutions have you ever achieved? There is a direct correlation between the number of 'yes's' that a group of people will offer and the length of time between New Year and when you actually ask that question. By June only a handful of people will say that they have made any progress, and by September people will not even admit to having made one! However, there is a far more successful approach to setting goals – read on to find out.

## Benefits of goal-setting

Setting goals at work and in other aspects of your life has many benefits which relate to time management.

- It helps you to identify what tasks you need to do.
- It helps you to decide which requests to say 'yes' or 'no' to
- It gives you a sense of being in control.
- Achieving goals gives you a feeling of success and spurs you on to achieve more.

**Where next?**

*Give Me Time*, Mind Gym, published by Time Warner Books, 2006.

## Top tip

Scheduling time for pleasurable activities and rest is just as important as setting time for tasks – if you don't have time to recharge your batteries, how much energy can you expect to have left for the big projects?

**Mike Phillips, Freelance Trainer and Consultant**

## Roles and goals

Let's look first at the various roles that you fulfil in your everyday life. Use the sample list presented here to select all of the roles that apply to you and write them in the numbered table.

Estimate, in a typical week, what percentage of your usable time you spend in each role. (Assume there are 100 usable hours per week – just over 14 per day for the seven days in the week. Shade in the proportion of the space to reflect this for each role.)

For example, shade 25% of the 'Now' cell if you spend 25 hours per week in the role of 'manager'.

Sample list of roles:

| | | |
|---|---|---|
| Manager | Friend | Parent |
| Colleague | Business owner | Grandparent |
| PA/secretary | Spouse/partner | Son/daughter |
| Coach/mentor | Carer | Looking after yourself |
| Governor | Trustee | Voluntary worker |

| | | Now | Future |
|---|---|---|---|
| Manager | 1 | | |
| | 2 | | |
| | 3 | | |
| | 4 | | |
| | 5 | | |

Consider the following questions.

- Did you spend time in each of the areas in which you wanted to spend time?
- In which areas did you spend too much time?
- Which roles would you like to have that don't currently feature in your life?
- Which roles would you like to get rid of?

Next steps:

- Capture in your action plan (see page 29) what you have to do to get rid of the roles you no longer want (for example, advise the board that you will be stepping down as a trustee in *x* months' time).
- Exclude those roles on which you choose not to spend time.
- Shade in the spaces under the 'Future' column to reflect the proportion of weekly time you want to spend in each role.

## Setting a goal for each role

State the goal in terms of what you want to do/be/ achieve/have/feel. Make this statement as specific as possible. For example:

- I want to spend 50% of my time managing people.
- I want to have at least three hours of fun time with my children each week.
- I want to leave the office by 5pm four days out of five, having completed all of my actions.

Assign a timeframe to each goal. For example:

- I want to spend 50% of my time managing people as from 18 July.

Check the feasibility of each goal:

- Is this goal within my control?
- Is it personally motivating?

If you find that you cannot answer 'Yes' to each of the feasibility questions, either review and amend the goal so that it does pass the feasibility test, or consider what other steps you need to take to overcome some of the challenges. For example, if it is not completely within your control, who else do you need to influence so that they support you?

**Top tip**

Keep a record of your goals close to hand and remind yourself of them regularly.

**Top tip**

Tell others your goals – they will help you, and you will be more motivated to achieve them.

**Julia Cawthorne, Funding and PR Manager, GFS Platform**

## Case study

Louise uses a technique to turn a time management problem into a goal. She thinks of an issue: *I'm always late for meetings* and asks herself some questions:
**1)** What would you like to happen instead of this challenge? *I'd like to be on time for every meeting, fully prepared and ready to contribute.*
**2)** What would that give you? *I'd feel relaxed. I think my manager would see me in a new, positive light and give me more opportunity to contribute.* **3)** Why is that important? *I would enjoy my job more and be in a better position to negotiate a promotion at the next staff reviews.*

At this stage you have decided the roles in your life to which you want to dedicate time. You have allocated specific amounts of time to each, and for each role you have defined what you want to achieve within a certain timeframe.

## Motivation to change

It is very easy for people who are on top of their time management to preach to those who are struggling about what they should be doing and why. However, the impetus to make lasting changes must come from within ourselves.

### Create a compelling goal

Typically, the motivation to change our habits is sparked off by a time management crisis: for example, perhaps we didn't complete the paperwork for a funding application in time, and consequently the project has been shelved. This sort of motivation will get you so far – to get away from the original problem – but over time the effect will weaken and you need to replace it with a compelling goal.

Try the technique shown in the case study using some of your own time management problems. Once you have created highly motivating goals, the following chapters will give you ideas to address the time management challenges.

# Chapter 3

# Managing tasks

*This chapter looks at some simple, proven techniques to help you manage your tasks. You will find practical and creative ways to overcome the personal time management challenges that you identified in chapter 1.*

## Identifying important tasks

> *'Things which matter most must never be at the mercy of things which matter least.'*
> *Johann Wolfgang von Goethe*

Here is an exercise to help you identify the tasks that matter.

1. Take one action on your 'to do' list and put it to test:

- Is this task important in helping you to achieve your objectives?
- Is this task urgent in that it needs to be done within the next 24 hours?

If you answer 'yes' to both of these questions, mark it '1'.

If you answer 'yes' to the first question and 'no' to the second, mark it '2'.

**Top tip**

Don't waste time on your in tray. Action every item – either bin it, do it then or put it in your diary for a future date and file it.

**Paul Matthews, External Affairs Manager, Young Enterprise North West**

**Top tip**

If you find that you tend to do the easiest tasks on your list first rather than the important tasks, put only two or three important tasks on the list. In this way, you have less chance of being distracted.

**Top tip**

Never fill your diary: schedule 50 to 60% of your time to allow for things that crop up – they always do!

**Cathy Shimmin, Senior Training Consultant, DSC**

If you answer 'no' to the first and 'yes' to the second question, mark it '3'.

If you answer 'no' to both questions, mark it '4'.

2. Put the task into the box marked '1' below.

3. Repeat parts 1 and 2 for all of the other tasks on your list.

| 1. Urgent and important | 2. Not urgent and important |
|---|---|
| 3. Urgent and not important | 4. Not urgent and not important |

What sort of tasks are in each of the boxes? Check them against the time management quadrant presented here.

4. The numbers of the boxes indicate the order in which you should address these tasks – 1, 2 and 3. The tasks which you have put in box 4 should be removed from your to do list. They have no relevance to your objectives and no time dimension.

5. Estimate how long it will take to do each of the tasks and plan them across your working week, prioritising the '1' tasks over the '2' tasks, and the '2' tasks over the '3' tasks.

The following time management quadrant (based on Stephen Covey's from *The 7 Habits of Highly Effective People*) shows the types of situations which come under the four headings. It also shows the possible consequences when most of your tasks fall in any one sector.

**Time management quadrant**

| 1. Urgent and important | 2. Not urgent but important |
|---|---|
| ▦ genuine crises<br>▦ pressing problems<br>▦ projects or work driven by deadlines<br>▦ firefighting<br><br>Consequences:<br>▦ burnout<br>▦ stress | ▦ planning<br>▦ relationship building<br>▦ creative thinking – new opportunities<br>▦ preventing crises, projecting<br>▦ professional knowledge<br><br>Consequences:<br>▦ vision<br>▦ perspective<br>▦ control<br>▦ balance |
| 3. Not important but urgent | 4. Not important and not urgent |
| ▦ interruptions<br>▦ some calls<br>▦ some mail<br>▦ some reports<br>▦ unprepared meetings<br><br>Consequences:<br>▦ out of control situation<br>▦ short-term focus<br>▦ victimised feeling | ▦ irrelevant mail and calls<br>▦ trivia<br>▦ unproductive activities<br><br>Consequences:<br>▦ irresponsibility<br>▦ dependence on others |

In this quadrant, sector 2 – not urgent but important – is the key sector on which to concentrate.

It may be that, having done this exercise, you can see that there is no possibility of fitting all of the tasks into a working week. Look at the sections on page 18 to find further help.

Remember: if you want time to relax, think, plan or do whatever else is important to you – plan it!

> 'The key is not to prioritise your schedule but to schedule your priorities.'
>
> *Stephen Covey*

**Where next?**

*Achieve,*
**M Butcher, published by DSC, 2003.**

## Top tip

When you need to goad yourself in action, try creating a holiday deadline. For example, make a commitment to friends, family or colleagues which will force you to finish work at a set time.

## Top tip

Use your diary as more than just an appointments-with-other-people book: make appointments with yourself. Build in your 'to do' list and planning and thinking time.

**Cathy Shimmin, Senior Training Consultant, DSC**

# Overcommitted: the four 'A's technique

You agreed to go to a meeting on behalf of your manager. You have a 'to do' list dating back three months. You have volunteered to sit with a new colleague while they make their first fundraising calls, and on top of that, you are facing a report deadline. Which do you do first?

The first step is to admit that you cannot meet all of these commitments personally. The second step is to apply the four 'A's:

- **A**ct on it
- **A**sk someone else to do it
- **A**xe it
- **A**lter it – that is, the timeframe or size of the task.

Scan your 'to do' list and pick out the important actions which only you can do and which are time critical. Assess how much time they will take versus how much time you have. If the time needed exceeds the time that you have, use the other three 'A's.

- Could someone else in the team go to the meeting? If not, could you go to part of it rather than the whole meeting?
- Are you the only person who could help the new colleague with their first calls, or could that task be delegated? Would you be able to spend 10 minutes with them at the beginning and come back later in the day or week, having completed your other tasks?
- Check whether the report deadline can be extended. If not, could someone else do it or help you to do it? What are the implications of missing the deadline?

## Anticipating the unexpected – or thunderbolts

There are two approaches you may take.

1  Look out for the unexpected – while some challenges may be truly unexpected, such as a fire which forces you out of your office, others may be anticipated with a bit of clever planning.
2  Build in a time buffer – It is very tempting to plan every second of your day in the belief that success is measured by the amount of things that you tick off. However, this approach leaves no room for unforeseen important and urgent tasks.

## Underestimating the size of the task

Again, there are two elements to this challenge: prevention and cure.

### Prevention

If you want to know how long a task will take you to do, ask someone who knows you! Research has shown that other people are much more accurate at estimating how long you will take. A good benchmark is to add 20% to your own estimates.

### Cure

When you are faced with a task which clearly cannot be done in the time that you have, try this approach.

■  Break it down into individual action chunks.
■  Decide which ones are critical to achieving the task and which ones could be removed.
■  Allocate an amount of time to each of the critical tasks.
■  Assess whether anyone else could help with any of the critical tasks.
■  If the total time still exceeds the time available, ask whether the timescales can be moved.

**Case study**

Jill is the personnel manager of a busy charity. She has a full workload which includes recruitment, overseeing staff reviews and supporting the chief executive. She has noticed that in January each year there is a rise in the number of people who want to talk about their career prospects. To allow time for these unscheduled conversations, Jill avoids committing to tight deadlines on other projects at this time of year.

## Where to start

Anywhere would be a good start when the task list seems huge. A long and ever-increasing task list can be truly overwhelming and virtually immobilise us. These steps will get you back into productive action.

### Action checklist

❑ Reduce your 'to do' list to no more than seven items by deleting unimportant tasks and applying the four 'A's to the remainder.

❑ Group together similar tasks – for example, list all the phone calls under the heading 'Phone calls'.

❑ Work out how much time each task will take, add 20%, and calculate the total. Plan your prioritised tasks over a realistic time span.

❑ As your first activity, choose a task which is important and urgent and which you feel competent in tackling. This will help to get you into a good flow.

❑ Strictly limit the amount of time that you will spend on each task and stick to that time limit.

❑ Stick to one job at a time and only move onto the next once you have reached the time limit that you have set, or when you have completed the task, if that is earlier.

### Procrastination

When you find yourself thinking yet again, 'Oh, another day won't make much difference', for that challenging proposal try this approach.

■ Ask yourself, 'What is stopping me from doing this?' List the reason(s).

■ If the answer is 'It's because I need . . .', get what you need!

■ If the answer is 'It's difficult', 'It's boring', create a compelling outcome (see chapter 2 on creating compelling future goals).

---

**Top tip**

Keep sticky notes and a pen to hand to make the most of waiting times or delays. Sticky notes are handy because you can place them in a useful spot when you get back to base!

**Roisin Kelly, Skills Development Officer, NICVA**

---

**Top tip**

If you are struggling to compose a report, reply to an email or create a proposal, write down anything and then edit it. Waiting for perfection to form in your mind is a great time-waster.

Next, break the task down into smaller bite-sized chunks and tackle one of those – then the next, and so on.

## Crises

How do you know when you are dealing with a true crisis? This sample model will guide you through the criteria and help you to deal with a genuinely challenging situation.

| Crisis | Your photocopier is broken. |
|---|---|
| Impact | No handouts for the trustees' meeting which is due to begin in 15 minutes. |
| Options | ■ Hold the meeting without handouts.<br>■ Delay the meeting.<br>■ Show the information via computer presentation.<br>■ Get the photocopying done at the shop around the corner.<br>■ Put the key information on a flipchart.<br>■ Share the single set of notes at the meeting.<br>■ Any other options? |
| Resources | ■ Photocopying shop.<br>■ PowerPoint presentation.<br>■ Personal assistant, who could write up key information on flipchart.<br>■ IT personnel.<br>■ Administration staff to make phone calls.<br>■ Any other resources? |
| Plan | ■ Check with trustees whether a delay would be acceptable.<br>■ Check if an IT person is available to help set up the computer presentation.<br>■ Phone photocopying shop to check how long copying would take. |
| Action | Put the plan into effect. |

**Top tip** 🔆

Treat email as a specific activity. Allocate an amount of time to it and schedule it into your day.

**Top tip** 🔆

When faced with each decision, ask yourself: 'What other information do I need to make a decision now?' If you can, make the decision immediately and move on.

**Julia Cawthorne, Funding and PR Manager, GFS Platform**

## Email checklist

Here are some key principles to manage emails and to stop them managing your time.

- ❏ Turn the message alert function off.
- ❏ Plan set times in your day to check emails.
- ❏ Use your signature function to let others know when you check emails.
- ❏ If you have to think hard about how to word your message on email, you probably should be using a different, more appropriate medium.
- ❏ Use rule settings to file incoming messages automatically.
- ❏ Use the subject line to communicate the action required of the recipient.
- ❏ Aim to 'handle' each message only once. Delete it immediately if it is no longer needed, deal with it if a quick response is possible, or delay and move it to a 'pending' folder if you need to do some more work before responding.

## Decision making

Consider your response to these questions.

- ▦ What sandwich would you like to have for lunch today?
- ▦ What would you do if you were offered your manager's job today?
- ▦ What holidays will you take this year?
- ▦ Which colour office chair would you like?

Did you take the same amount of time over each decision?

You will have different decision-making processes for a wide range of scenarios. Where you recognise that the impact of the decision is very small, you can make a quick decision. However, you can lose valuable time deliberating over a relatively insignificant decision because you don't acknowledge that the impact is small.

# Chapter 4

# Managing people

*This chapter looks at pre-emptive and real-time approaches to situations where you need others' help and input, and they need yours. The skill in dealing with people and time management challenges is achieving the task while maintaining the relationship.*

## Interruptions

Wouldn't it be great to work without interruption – or would it? Think back over the last week and recall the times when you were interrupted. Were they all unwelcome interruptions, or were you glad of that break? Interruptions can bring much-needed respite from an arduous task, useful information, a sense of importance and of being needed, as well as a sense of frustration. How you deal with them sets the standard for future situations.

### *Let them know*

What can you do to let others know when you need to work without interruptions? Pick out from this list the ideas which would be practical in your work environment.

■ Close the office door and put a sign up, indicating when you will be free to talk again.

**Top tip**

When others say that their request is 'urgent', take time to question and understand the real deadlines – and the consequences of any delay, if any.

**Jamie Wilcox, Chief Executive, Volunteer Centre Kensington and Chelsea**

- Set your phone to 'divert', with a message saying when you will be available.
- Put a 'flag' or other indicator on your desk to let colleagues know that you need to concentrate.
- Speak to your team or colleagues in advance, advising them that you will be working on your own between *x* and *y* o'clock.
- Fix a set time each week when you are out of reach and advertise it.

## How to deal with interruptions

This is your opportunity to educate and develop others. The key is to assess what is needed quickly and respond in a way that encourages the future behaviour that you want.

| Need | Response |
|------|----------|
| Your expertise | - If you can deal with it quickly, do. If not, propose a better time to talk about it. |
| Reassurance | - 'I feel that you always make good decisions. Don't worry about running them past me.' |
| Permission | - If it is not a good time for you, ask if you can discuss the situation at a better time. <br> - If permission is not actually required, ask questions in such a way that the person can see that they have reached the right solution without your help. |
| A signature | - Have a labelled in-tray for documents requiring signature. |
| A chat | - 'I would love to catch up but don't have much time at the moment/during work. Could we meet up at lunch/after work?' |

## Lengthy conversations and rambling meetings

This is where you need to regain control of the situation. The following formula for avoiding lengthy conversations is particularly useful:

*Summarise + propose next steps + check agreement*

For example:

*It sounds as though there are a lot of changes in the fundraising team. I would find it really useful to see a short bulleted summary on email. Could you do that for me? Thanks. (Close the conversation.)*

*This has been really useful. Perhaps we should have a 10-minute catch-up every month. Let's put it in the diary now. Is that OK with you?*

> **Where next?**
>
> *NLP at Work*, S Knight, published by Nicholas Brealey, 2002.

Every meeting should have the following elements.

| Format | Example |
|---|---|
| Agreed outcome(s) | Draft a programme of community events for 2010. |
| An agenda which supports the outcome | ▪ Funds available to support the programme.<br>▪ Summary of previous events which were successful.<br>▪ Brainstorm to generate new ideas.<br>▪ Decide on the best ideas from these options.<br>▪ Agree next steps. |
| A clear and distinct role for each person | ▪ Facilitator – to structure the meeting, keep it on track for time and outcome.<br>▪ 2009 programme manager – to present previous successes and funding structure; participate in brainstorming.<br>▪ Events coordinators (2) – to help the group to understand how the events would be deployed and the obstacles to be aware of; participate in brainstorming.<br>▪ Marketing manager – to be actively involved in the brainstorming session; start to understand the marketing requirements. |

## Top tip

If the outcome can be achieved in a short meeting, consider holding it in a place with no chairs, tea or biscuits. This will ensure that the meeting is quick.

**Jamie Wilcox, Chief Executive, Volunteer Centre Kensington and Chelsea**

## Exercise

Think of a meeting which you are running or one to which you have been invited.

Write down the outcome, agenda and roles for each person invited, in that order.

Does the agenda support the outcome?

Does everyone invited have a specific and distinct role?

In what other ways could the outcome be achieved?

This exercise is a good checklist for every meeting in which you are involved.

## Handling others' expectations

### Lots of people need you

It can be immensely flattering to be needed by a large number of individuals. However, it can be exhausting and frustrating. If your main purpose is to lead, manage and generally support many individuals, you will need to do so proactively, or commit yourself to a life of reacting.

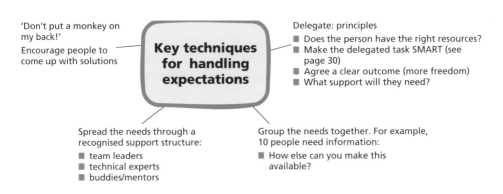

'Don't put a monkey on my back!'
Encourage people to come up with solutions

**Key techniques for handling expectations**

Delegate: principles
- Does the person have the right resources?
- Make the delegated task SMART (see page 30)
- Agree a clear outcome (more freedom)
- What support will they need?

Spread the needs through a recognised support structure:
- team leaders
- technical experts
- buddies/mentors

Group the needs together. For example, 10 people need information:
- How else can you make this available?

## People who disregard your time

In addition to the approaches you have looked at in the rest of this chapter, there are times when a more forthright tack needs to be taken.

The feedback model below gives us a simple structure to tackle persistent offenders. The beauty of it is that, when used well, it can help you to maintain a good relationship with the other person. The SBI model stands for Situation, Behaviour, Impact, and the following examples will help you to see it in action.

| Situation | Behaviour | Impact |
|---|---|---|
| I notice that you write a lot of emails in your job. | While you are doing this you often ask me whether they sound ok or not. | I am finding it difficult to concentrate to produce daily reports and I am getting sidetracked by our conversations. I have now missed quite a few deadlines and it doesn't reflect well on me or the team. |
| Recently, while you've been working on the grant application, you have needed quite a lot of input from me. | What has happened is that you have asked for this help as you work through the document, rather than in one hit. | The problem it is causing me is that I can't anticipate how much of my time you need and when. Consequently, I am getting behind on my own work. |

Let's look briefly now at the other side of managing people and time.

## Top tip

**When you ask for five minutes of someone's time, make sure that you only take five minutes, or they may be reluctant to help you the next time.**

## Getting time with busy people

A good principle to grasp is that of 'What's in it for me?'. If you can sell the benefit to the other person of giving you some of their time, you are far more likely to win it.

For example:

> *'If I could have 20 minutes of your time today, I could pull together the draft strategy paper which you are planning to present to the trustees at next month's meeting.'*

You can draw on the approaches just discussed that you use when others want your time.

| Problem | Approach |
|---|---|
| Interruptions | ■ Find out the times when they are accessible.<br>■ Make sure that they are the right person for you to approach for help, not just the nearest. |
| Lengthy conversations | ■ Summarise your situation to date.<br>■ Propose the action that you want them to take.<br>■ Check that they are happy to provide this and the timescales. |
| Rambling or unnecessary meetings | ■ Ensure that the outcome of the meeting is of value to them.<br>■ Be prepared to accommodate their other time commitments. It may mean structuring the agenda to suit them.<br>■ Clearly communicate their role in the meeting. |
| Lots of people need you | ■ Gather others who also may need time from this busy person, so they can speak once to a group rather than several times to individuals.<br>■ Approach them with a proposal or solution rather than a problem. |

# Chapter 5

# Take action: a plan

*This chapter helps you to turn those ideas into your personal time management plan.*

## Create an action log

Throughout this book you will have gathered actions which could give you back control of your time. Some may have a significant impact (High = H), and others may make little difference (Low = L). The following table shows the impact rating of some examples used in the book and in which chapters the relevant techniques are outlined. Create a similar table outlining your actions and their impact levels.

| Action | Impact: High/Medium/Low (H/M/L) |
|---|---|
| Advise the board that, having considered my 'roles and goals', I will be stepping down at the end of the month. (Chapter 2) | M |
| Every Friday I will create a work plan for the following week using the 4 quadrant matrix. (Chapter 3) | H |
| I will use a benefit statement when asking for time with others. (Chapter 4) | M |
| I will use a flag on my desk to let others know when I need to work without interruptions. (Chapter 4) | L |

In turn, consider how much of a time saving each of these actions would give you. Score each as H, M or L.

Those which you have marked as high impact deserve to be prioritised over the medium and low impact actions. Take action now to make them happen!

What if it isn't that easy? What if stepping down from the staff council sets off a round of meetings which consume even more of your time than the original task? It's time to 'SMART' your actions.

### SMART

| | |
|---|---|
| **S** (specific) | I will step down as a member of the staff council. |
| **M** (measurable) | I will no longer receive emails inviting me to the meetings and I will have no outstanding actions from previous meetings. |
| **A** (achievable) | I will find a replacement for my position, someone whom I know has expressed an interest in the past. |
| **R** (realistic) | I will give the team notice at this week's meeting and be prepared to take part until the end of this month. |
| **T** (timeframed) | As of 1 March I will have handed over fully to the new team member or passed on responsibility for recruiting someone to the council. |

As you can see, the SMART approach makes your action much more likely to happen. It forces you to decide on an endpoint and to be creative, practical and action-oriented.

For each of your high-impact actions, run the SMART approach. Using a table can help break it down.

---

## Top tip

Once you've decided on new habits, be patient with yourself – remember that it takes time to develop one (approximately three weeks) and it's natural to slip back into your old way of doing things. If that's what happens, don't beat yourself up over it, just try again. Like the old adage: if at first you don't succeed, try, try again.

**Mike Phillips,
Freelance Trainer
and Consultant**

## Create new habits

### Embed a brand new habit

If you want to make a new habit stick, wrap it in an existing habit. What do we mean by this?

Think of a time when you had to take medication. You make a conscious effort at first, but after a few days began to forget to take it. If you make it part of the routine where you make a hot drink in the morning and a glass of water at night, it is far more likely to become embedded.

## Use existing practices

I have heard many time management delegates, including myself, say 'I work best when I have a looming deadline.' Many of us also experience this when we are going on holiday and manage to complete an enormous number of tasks just before we go.

For many it would be a quantum leap to change this practice which, after all, has served us well for so long. Instead you could work with this dynamic.

For example: you are organising a seminar to take place on 11 March.

- You have identified that the key tasks are to book a suitable venue, secure speakers, invite guests and provide handouts.
- Providing handouts is the last task in the series and it would be tempting to leave this until 9 or 10 March, if you have other work to do.

Instead, you commit to deliver the handouts to the venue by 8 March – creating a deadline for yourself, but which is well within the project deadline.

**Case study**

John vowed to look at emails only three times a day and to switch off the email alert button. Typically, he has a teabreak at 11am and at 3pm and stops for lunch at 12.30. One morning he switched off the email alert button and only checked his emails around those three breaks.

## Review your plan

You have armed yourself with useful techniques and tips to manage your priorities and other commitments. However, you can be sure that your scenario and the demands on your time will change regularly.

**Top tip**

Use the Stop, Start, Continue model as a powerful, quick and easy way to ensure that your time management stays on track.

**Cathy Shimmin, Senior Training Consultant, DSC**

**Where next?**

DSC runs several personal development courses, including **Improving Your Time Management**. To find out more go to www.dsc.org.uk/Training/Personal development

| Task | From when |
|---|---|
| *Stop*<br>I will stop looking at emails as soon as they arrive. | Today |
| I will stop interrupting others for a 'quick chat' and keep the conversation for a coffee break instead. | Immediately |
| *Start*<br>I will start planning weekly and review the plan before I go home each day. | End of this week |
| I will prioritise my 'to do' list and reward myself for sticking to it, rather than do the easy things first. | Immediately |
| I will aim to handle each piece of paper only once.<br>I will structure my meetings using the outcome, agenda and roles format. | Team meeting, 8 February |
| *Continue*<br>I will keep a list of both my work and home life commitments in one book. | |

Approach each challenge with the knowledge that you do have choices about how you spend your time. Bolstered by the range of techniques and strategies which you have covered, you can start reaping the benefits of being in control.